XF        Herz, Henry, author.
HER        When
           penny
312016    and Ha

D0844509

ST. MARY PARISH LIBRARY
FRANKLIN, LOUISIANA

# When You Give an
# Imp a Penny

By Henry, Josh, and Harrison Herz

Illustrated by Abigail Larson

**PELICAN PUBLISHING COMPANY**
GRETNA 2016

Copyright © 2016
By Henry Herz
All rights reserved

*The word "Pelican" and the depiction of a pelican are
trademarks of Pelican Publishing Company, Inc., and are
registered in the U.S. Patent and Trademark Office.*

ISBN 9781455621446
E-book ISBN 9781455621453

*This is a work of fiction. All characters and events portrayed in this book are fictional, and
any resemblance to real incidents, people, or imps is purely coincidental.*

Printed in Malaysia

Published by Pelican Publishing Company, Inc.
1000 Burmaster Street, Gretna, Louisiana 70053

*With gratitude to Laura Numeroff, my parents, and the Author of all things*
—Henry Herz

When you give an imp a penny,
he's going to ask for a coin bag.

If you give him a coin bag, he'll probably want a shovel. Then he'll bury the coin bag for safekeeping.

He'll ask you for a pebble to mark his buried treasure.

When he follows you inside, he'll track dirt into your house. So, you'll ask him to clean it up.

He'll sweep near the door. Then he'll
sweep by the fireplace.

He'll accidentally catch the broom on fire. So, you'll dunk the broom in a bucket of water.

He'll want to make you a new broom.
So . . . he'll pull straw from your mattress.
Then he'll ask for some twine.

He'll tie new straw on the broomstick.

Then he'll hand you the broom with
an embarrassed smile.

With some spare twine, he'll braid a collar for your cat. The cat will hiss, but he'll insist. When the cat flees, it will probably run through the dirt pile.

So . . . he'll have to give the cat a bath.
The cat will hiss, but he'll insist.
Then he'll have to mop the floor.

All this work will make him hungry. So he'll ask for
an apple. You'll give him your last one.

When treated with kindness, imps gain the
power to conjure treasure.

He'll probably thank you with gold coins. *Poooof!*

All those coins will remind him about his coin bag.

And chances are, if he digs
up his coin bag, he's going to
ask you for another penny.

# NOTE

Brownies may enjoy tidying up around the house, but when you're an imp like me, nothing is more fun than making a little mischief. I like humans, and playing pranks on them is how I show my affection.

Can't find that missing sock? Wondering why the toys aren't where you left them? Don't know how shirts come out of the dryer inside out? You may have an imp living with you. It might even be me!